Tell Time
with Turtles

By Melissa McDonnell

Gareth Stevens
Publishing

Please visit our website, www.garethstevens.com. For a free color catalog of all our high-quality books, call toll free 1-800-542-2595 or fax 1-877-542-2596.

Library of Congress Cataloging-in-Publication Data

McDonnell, Melissa.
Tell time with turtles / Melissa McDonnell.
     p. cm. — (Animal math)
Includes index.
ISBN 978-1-4339-5676-8 (pbk.)
ISBN 978-1-4339-5677-5 (6-pack)
ISBN 978-1-4339-5674-4 (library binding)
1. Time—Miscellanea—Juvenile literature. 2. Turtles—Miscellanea—Juvenile literature. I. Title.
QB209.5.M33 2012
529'.2—dc22

                              2011001684

First Edition

Published in 2012 by
Gareth Stevens Publishing
111 East 14th Street, Suite 349
New York, NY 10003

Designer: Haley W. Harasymiw
Editor: Therese M. Shea

Photo credits: Cover, pp. 1, 4, 5, 7, 9, 11, 13, 15, 17, 19, 21 Shutterstock.com.

Printed in the United States of America

CPSIA compliance information: Batch #CR217260GS: For further information contact Gareth Stevens, New York, New York at 1-800-542-2595.

Contents

Boldface words appear in the glossary.

Time for Turtles!

There are about 300 kinds of turtles. Some live on land. Some live in water. It's time to see turtles at the zoo!

Shells

All turtles have shells. A turtle hides its head inside its shell to keep safe.

This turtle hid at 9:00.

Food

Turtles don't have teeth. A turtle uses its **beak** to tear food. Turtles have strong **jaws**, too.

These turtles ate at 10:00.

9

Turtles eat plants. Most eat animals such as bugs and worms, too. Sea turtles eat fish and other sea animals.

This sea turtle ate at 10:30.

11

Eggs and Babies

Turtles come from eggs. Most mother turtles dig a hole and lay their eggs in it.

A mother turtle laid eggs at 11:00. Point to the clock that shows 11:00.

13

Baby turtles break out of their eggs. Then they look for food. Some crawl to water.

This baby turtle came out of its egg at 12:30. Point to the clock that shows 12:30.

15

Staying Warm

Turtles are **reptiles**. They need the sun to stay warm. Land turtles lay in the sun on cold days.

This turtle crawled into the sun at 1:00. It stayed there for 1 hour. What time was it then?

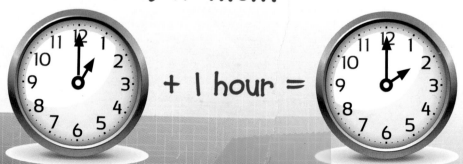

+ 1 hour =

17

Speedy Leatherbacks

Leatherback sea turtles are the fastest turtles. They spend nearly their whole lives in water.

The clock below shows when this leatherback turtle came up for air. What time was it?

19

Slow Tortoises

Tortoises live only on land. Many move very slowly.

This tortoise started to walk at 3:00. It walked for 1 hour. What time did it stop?

Glossary

beak: a part of the mouth that sticks out on some animals and is used to tear food

jaw: one of the two bones in which teeth are set

reptile: an animal that has scales, breathes air, and lays eggs. Turtles, snakes, crocodiles, and lizards are reptiles.

Answer Key

page 12: top clock   **page 18:** 2:30

page 14: bottom clock   **page 20:** 4:00

page 16: 2:00

For More Information

Books

Dowdy, Penny. *Time*. New York, NY: Crabtree Publishing, 2009.

Murphy, Patricia J. *Telling Time with Puppies and Kittens*. Berkeley Heights, NJ: Enslow Publishers, 2007.

Websites

All About Turtles
octopus.gma.org/turtles/index.html
Learn about different kinds of turtles.

Math: Telling Time
classroom.jc-schools.net/basic/math-time.html
This site has many links to games about time.

Time Travel: Learn to Tell Time!
www.abcya.com/telling_time.htm
Play a game using two kinds of clocks.

Index